POWWOW

Written by Vanessa York
Photography by Martha Cooper

North America

Native American Carla Monson is Mohawk. She lives in the big city of New York, but she has another home on the Kahnawake (*Gah na WA geh*) reserve in Canada. She respects her Mohawk heritage and enjoys joining in Kahnawake's annual powwow.

respect to place a high value on something

Contents

Powwow

My name is Carla Monson. I live with my parents, my sister Laurie, and my little brother Lawrence in Brooklyn, which is part of New York City. My mother is a Mohawk from the Kahnawake Mohawk Nation in Canada. Every summer we visit our grandparents and cousins there.

Our cousins on the reserve there like to play baseball, so we always practice before we visit.

reserve   reservation; the land of a Native American community

We go to Kahnawake every summer.

Sometimes, Grandma comes to visit us in Brooklyn.

Across the road from my grandparents' house in Kahnawake is the St. Lawrence River. Mohawks have been traveling on the river for hundreds of years. Some Mohawks patrol the river, watching out for pollution and harm to wildlife. My cousins and I like to paddle our kayaks for fun.

Maybe one day, we will be like Alwyn Morris and win a gold medal for kayaking at the Olympics.

When Alwyn Morris received his gold medal at the Olympics in 1984, he held up an eagle feather to honor his Mohawk heritage.

Every summer in Kahnawake, people from many different tribes gather for a powwow. There is always music and dancing at the powwow. There are dancing competitions, and everyone is welcome to take part in the inter-tribal dancing that takes place. There are many arts and crafts for sale, as well as plenty of delicious food, such as venison and fry bread.

Laurie and I wear the beautiful, colorful Mohawk clothing, called regalia, that Aunt Selma made for us.

fry bread   flat bread that is fried in a pan

Tips for Attending a Powwow

- When the eagle staff is brought in during the grand entry, everyone stands to show respect.

- Pointing is considered rude. Instead of pointing, purse your lips and either move your eyes or nod your head in the direction of what it is you wish to point out.

- Do not bother the performers or stand in front of people who are getting ready to dance or sing.

- Ask permission before photographing anyone.

Laurie and I have fun getting ready.

A special part of my regalia is a fan made of duck feathers that my cousin Tionahose (*Jon a HO zay*) gave me.

In the inter-tribal dance, I dance to the music of the drum and hold my fan up high on the important beats.

All too soon, our trip is over, and it's time to go back to the city. Before we go, Grandma shows us her collection of old family photographs and tells us about the people in them. Saying goodbye to everyone is hard, but Tionahose has promised to visit me in Brooklyn soon.

When I'm at Kahnawake, it feels like home, and I never want to leave. However, after a few days in Brooklyn and seeing all my city friends again, I'm at home there, too!

What stories have you been told about old family photographs?

 Explore North America

The continent of North America extends from the Canadian Arctic, far in the north, to Mexico in the south. It includes many kinds of landforms, from ice caps to forests, mountains, plains, and deserts.

The Rocky Mountains link Canada, the United States, and Mexico. The Rockies stretch for 3,000 miles, from the Yukon in Canada down through the United States to Mexico.

This picture, taken from space at night, makes it easy to see the most heavily populated areas of North America.

landforms   the natural features that make up
            the surface of the earth

Niagara Falls form a natural boundary between Canada and the United States. Niagara Falls are made up of two large waterfalls and one small one.

On the Go!

What is the largest city in Canada?
Go to page 18

Which sport was first played by Native Americans?
Go to page 21

How many people live in Nunavut?
Go to page 23

ARCTIC OCEAN

Alaska,
U.S.A.

CANADA

Ottawa

Washington,
D.C.

UNITED STATES OF AMERICA

ATLANTIC OCEAN

MEXICO

Mexico City

Hawaii,
U.S.A.

PACIFIC OCEAN

Using the Land

Most people in North America live in cities, but farming is still a very important activity. Much of what is grown in North America feeds North Americans, but a lot of produce is also exported.

The United States has huge cattle ranches and vast cornfields. Canada's great prairies east of the Rocky Mountains contain 75 percent of the nation's farmland. Only about one-fifth of Mexico's land is suitable for farming. Corn is the most common crop.

A worker nets fish at a Canadian salmon farm. Salmon farming is a growing industry in Canada.

export   to send goods to another country for sale

A cowboy herds cattle in Yucatan, Mexico. Beef and dairy cattle are raised in many areas of North America.

Cornfields in Ohio, U.S.A. Corn, or maize, has been harvested in North America for 10,000 years. It is used for a wide variety of food and manufacturing purposes.

Big Cities

North America has some of the world's largest cities. Mexico City, the capital of Mexico, has a population of more than eight million people. Washington, D.C., the capital of the United States, is home to diplomats from all over the world.

Ottawa is the capital of Canada. It is a beautiful city on the banks of the Ottawa River. The largest and most diverse city in Canada is Toronto. More than half of the people who live in Toronto were born outside Canada.

Downtown Toronto is the center of Canada's financial and communications industries.

diverse widely varied

The 150-foot-tall Monument to Independence is one of Mexico City's best-known landmarks.

New York, with more than seven million people, is the largest city in the United States. Millions of tourists visit each year to see such famous sights as the Empire State Building.

First Nations

The borders between Canada, the United States, and Mexico are only a few hundred years old. Native Americans have lived in North America for thousands of years.

There are many different tribes, or nations, of Native Americans. Members of a tribe share the same land, language, customs, and beliefs.

The ancestors of the Pueblo nation built this city in the southern desert regions of New Mexico.

Lacrosse was played by Native Americans before Europeans arrived in North America.

Native American farmers were the first to grow crops such as beans, squash, potatoes, tomatoes, and corn. Now these vegetables are grown all over the world.

Mexican Indian weavers use brightly colored patterns. Each region in Mexico has its own patterns.

In the past, some tribes, such as the Iroquois, lived mainly by farming. Tribes of the Plains, such as the Sioux, lived by hunting bison and gathering plants.

In the old days, when Native Americans were pushed from their homes by new settlers, the U.S. and Canadian governments set aside reservations for Native Americans to live on. These reservations were often too small to provide a traditional living such as hunting. Today, many Native Americans live and work in cities.

Industry provides many jobs for Native Americans.

traditional   usual; typical

These students are learning computer skills at school on the Spokane Indian Reservation.

Nunavut

Nunavut, Canada's newest territory, was created in 1999 after years of discussion between the Canadian government and the Inuit of the Nunavut area. The name *Nunavut* means "place of many fish" in the Inuktitut language. More than 28,000 people now live in Nunavut. Iqaluit, the capital city of Nunavut, has a population of about 6,000.

Iqaluit is the smallest capital in Canada, but it is the largest community in Nunavut.

What Do You Think?

1 Carla has two places where she feels at home. Tell about the place or places that you think of as home.

2 Carla admires the kayaker Alwyn Morris. Do you know of someone you wish you were like?

How do you show respect for your culture?

Index